ADVAN

MW00413463

"With all her senses alert, Kate Monahan is a poet of the Earth. Her intelligent poems yearn for a planet without hateful border stations, floating-trash islands, and elaborate human grief. We are just specks in the universe, but Monaghan's darkly bright poems tug us toward a renewable homeland."

—Henri Cole

"*Disputed Site* marks the arrival of an important new voice in American poetry. With lyricism informed by a truly humane spirit, and the clear-eyed inquisitiveness of a research scientist, Kate Monaghan is a poet of marvelous clarities and wide-world-faring vision. This generous collection— centered by *Oil Rig Sestinas*, which is one of the most important sequences of contemporary environmental poetry I have encountered—is intimate, meditative, complex, disturbing, revelatory. *Disputed Site* is a gorgeous and powerful debut."

—Bradford Morrow

"The soul must suffer the perils of its desires. Unsure of its origins, anxious as to its ending, it is, as Monaghan beautifully avows, "a hum that is moving"— moving among the debris of modernity, moving deeply into our menaced earth, moving with the dark companionship of history. But if there is peril, there is also the rich music of peril. *Disputed Site* amplifies this music beautifully. This is a splendid collection."

—Donald Revell

"Kate Monaghan is poet of elegance, acuity, verbal balance. She has a careful and observing eye, and fashions beautiful interiors of thought and feeling. She is also a poet of courage and compassion who can adapt her imaginative apparatus to some of the harshest realities of our world—foreign wars, fraught and dangerous borders, people condemned to brutal toil—and show us how our most intimate awareness of ourselves is inseparable from our moral and human responsibilities."

—Vijay Seshadri

"Planetary in ambition and alive with forms as varied as the world it portrays, Kate Monaghan's Disputed Site reminds us our bodies, no matter how much we may resist or deny, remain intrinsically linked to nature. We feel every rusted-out chassis, toxic ash heap, garbage patch, and oil spill as damage to our physical being, but with every wound, she leaves us an opportunity to heal. With every death—a chance to be reborn."

—Matthew Pennock, PhD, judge and
author of *The Miracle Machine* and *Sudden Dog*

DISPUTED SITE

POEMS

KATE MONAGHAN

Winner of the Gival Press Poetry Award

Arlington, Virginia

Published by Gival Press, an imprint of Gival Press, LLC.

For information please write:
Gival Press, LLC
P. O. Box 3812
Arlington, VA 22203
www.givalpress.com

First edition
ISBN: 978-1-940724-40-9
eISBN: 978-1-940724-41-6
Library of Congress Control Number: 2022944496

Cover art: Vladimir Fomin
Design by Ken Schellenberg

CONTENTS

for Jorie

CHASSIS EXCAVATION

America

If you had
a man,
        would you
give him a soul—

lying
on the table
cut and

        make it,
beg of him

to be good?

I was given
parents once, their
houses

        green from
timbers, cold
plateaus—

how light slit
                bedroom
floorboards
over decades, long
                surface thinly

altering

as one recalls
there is no
history

not even
          yours,
behind bushes,
                    the glass he built
the yard

and on,
without them—

was it the quiet
made them—
                    always thinking
of the war? in such

stately, blameless
houses, with no

politics
unto themselves

At the Hotel

Where substances form
at the mouth.

Swept for contaminants
there is no cause

arriving at only
the odd-numbered
floors.

Solution:
between two borders, a protocol
of final bubbling
over

and we adjust
in secret: move.

Order
the stubby doctor
to bedside over
her o-ring lips

(the cells sweat
beads
when not fed)

and the quiet

each time she gets well

each time she gets well
we receive
one gift.

Desire

A desire is a root
finding its way
in the water;
a desire is a fin
coursing
through all the extra
of your ways.

A way
is a plaintiff. A point
is all that rests there
seething.
The bow of the cart
and the rutted road
make
their gauge.

Are we now
as before
becoming?

There is no price
for this innocence.
Set on the waterways

a marshy
entrance
where the reedy
plants open
is where a boat
slips through

This is
lotus picking

stolen pastime
and she looks
into the water
after the storm
she looks
and the jade pin
falls

Chassis Excavation

Is there a customer here?
Up the Billy Budd hillside dark
marauding strangers stumble
back and forth, unsure
surely mongrel sorrel rats
apiece with five feathers,

draining out the mess
they've made of the beach
mean-times, the sudden
little paths between the house
and the great open
always empty sticks of reeds
protruding, the dry-spine
grasses wet for only a week
of summer.

Minnows
of the pond—dredged
right to the bottom, houses
here once were plentiful
as buggies. And yet it looks
like what we think of as nature,
if castrated and recast
in some acidic form. The rains
of ink wash, colliding

on this spit of land.
Tensile storms nearer now
between the ocean and the bay:
the way one can disappear
either up or down, when stability
begins to seem so hard to master
as if your foot kept

sinking through
the skin of the planet here
on marshland, as if the swans
skimming the dockside each day
no longer seemed complacent
and you followed them home
and from their nest they ran at you
and what is awful happened.

Perhaps there are good reasons
for doilies and cooking lessons.
For categories that hold the mind
with surface
and let you stay there.

The year of calculus I
remember staring at her face
and trying to take the derivative:
trying so hard even now
I think there must be some way
to do it. And they say
what we do is private.

And what we do now
with the brain: the operations,
and from the dune and mineral
patterns, these hints of what has come before
that is the same as this, that again
comes.

Concave/Convex

I believe I was raised somehow.

Don't we all?
So arid otherwise.

There was a fog
in the mountains. A dense one
that stuck to the bricks
when they fell off the truck
that was hauling us
down. We'd waited ages
to leave, milling around
for more passengers. I don't know
what those bricks were worth
but you can't buy a private trip
here no matter what
you try.

I think the jostle is just as well.

In 1,000 years I will be
a moss garden

till then, however, I limp
around as tender
as raked sand

Room

I was dreaming anxiety's
arrangement—unsure if we could call the wretched mind
its own distillation, or project it
as a film.

Unlike the tinderbox windows
slaking off outside's sand, I was cool
and damp and narrow-rimmed
as a lake reflection.

So what cavity
is there in image—for the lowing
mind in language
biding its time?

Weighing now
against the room:
fan still, the metal wires
ask, heat
spilling—

Forked branches can be cut
screaming for adversaries—
So I came streaming into vision

For the leaves to
            elongate to embitter strength
            and foreshorten
solid distances—

mirrored, mirroring
stripes—

it has to be

in the words, not in what they say

it has to be
soil for someone

who will not stay here long.

Sustain

The elaborate
grief—

quiet
as dunes, it shadows

our earth: where
the ridges spread, a solid
shape

grafted

tree: two apples
on one spring
stem

How to recite
it—
paper?

weather-beaten

did you think
we could survive, in just
attention

to the trusted places—

ceramic
and black grout:
its grains

of metal brightly—

games

repeated on a
spreading floor: but

there are not fathers
enough

for everyone: incumbent
earth

breaking open
what you revered—you

take
what you can, coming in
from the wild

there
she broke you: darling,

coming in—

you had to
follow, yet even she

succumbed. How far?

To the bank
of the river: maybe one
bend only

and the green grasses
never more lush

unfolding: take it
no distance:

how we are
orphaned still

Collage

There'll be killers in the grass tonight,

oh I know you're here
like always
erasures make the draughts
besieging

now's mirage Braque-built
display screen
sight-lines seamlessly and three
of one
lens looking

—   —   —

So collage then was a killer cutting
truth in two,
in two again

and after all
on most of us
we'll divide one eye

or one race, what's difference to dystopia
with arms tonight,
or with femme hair, what's
it measured up
to?

—   —   —

Not the built-up sky—dangling things
like
bragging streamers:

looking up at us, you
have-nots, at our riches

and pretend again
the text is you: no wonder you rebel
against those words

this weight
of the Latinate in your arms
when here only this dull rumor

and conquest of strength,
a parking lot
tired of translations.

Comb the beach again.

An engine running,
we exclaim our
disproportionate
divisions

and yet the unborn
become wet sun-lit days—

these unrepentant people

that come in shocks
to the mind
like rocks and bits of stone.

The Notion of Originality

Hey the warp
hey the warp is the graded chunk
that pulls you deftly—

wax
wax on the batter of the moon
and the tumble-down
tumble-down old
          random old wall

from the garden
the garden where the slice
of the melon grows to pulse
and droning

on to drown:
stuck to the water
and to die along it—both
the pull and the body
closing—sound

as if it were not water
as if it were not sound,
          light feet picking up
from the road as if
coming loose,
as if once and for all

THINGS CIRCULATE

Ceremonial Dialogue with the Feng Tripod

You bestow
>*a black jacket with embroidered hem*
>*red kneepads*

—these are the mines of hours
dipping tipping ever into enclaves
cascading from language
multiplied to hide repetitions,
the curt cup forms
eliding dialect.

Like a man who stands with his face to the wall what do you hear?

Here I am in my rock and cleft
here on the cushions here
on the floor. Inscription enacts
our thrones and our toes.
Words we are not tired to recite
even when there is no book-
burning we bury them
in the walls of the house.

You bestow
>*a scarlet demi-circlet*
>*a chime pennant*

—here is the gift of decoration
the wild articulate frenzy of things
given again to the page—given
first in bronze vessel's curve
given to me.

You bestow

  a bridle with bit and cheek pieces

Here *may we, sons of sons*
grandsons of grandsons—appreciate.

Like a man who stands with his face to the wall
what do you hear?

These are my bronze things
that I may serve

Touch Screen

I've stayed the same
by meaning to.
Most of the time
so overlaid
like a real thing.

The pond shows
painted, a glassy paste
as if I'd been
in the forest.

My tilting body seems
to mount its mechanics—

A deer
(as in language)
stepping forward

I turn and see
a slow handle lifting
out from the shadows

I was honed
then under pressure
to parse out this function

interest (a loop)

touching solid wildness

Drowned Man

The Mecox has never looked
so untroubled as when
she spoils her comb
across the paint
of this unevenly blue
chair. Its headache
rivulets of never-
time-for-hair
coil patiently

creating a place to sit.
The comments say, "try *rivers*
rather than *lakes*," from which
the water cannot escape.

Somewhere, the tides
cannot depart
this estuary
of looking—residing
and looking—
and where would
the slightest body go?

I mind the edges
of landscaping. The cultivated
speculation of a summer
divided into work-weeks
and years. But where are you
pasted into this story,
drowned man?

You are like the seaplane
descending, or the yard-worker
who left the garage unlocked

when the sailboat
was taken, and
if you were that man
who disappeared
and bought a ticket,
it was after stealing back money
that you had earned.

Borderland

i
Replace me.
SPEAK.

ii
Forgive
the broken yoke

strength's
rotten jaws

this dirty wisdom

when I clasped it—

iii
I wanted
to be free
of something—

what did I
do?

iv
The sting

of labor, (laced, unlaced)
strangeness

brewing on

abstraction—the sawing

of wings—the woodwork's ramp

and plastic
escalator—

replace me—
replace my parts

I'm gone

iv
there is no wood
in the orchard. There
is no water in the well. Covet
rains and the remaining
centers. We
shift in our places—recover

v
height:
the chambers—lie

through nights: the string
to draw

a magic circle:
safety

around
this little fear

The Leveling

When frenzied autumn
stirred winds
I was ready, perhaps
obsequious, gratuitous
with pauses
and alarms, the sleep
of the street
and the thrum
of elevators—
thus fearing
there would be more—
a sudden access
to perspective,
angle poised over you
from apartments
and balconies—
just looking.

Even you, the one
I share my corners
with, monotonous
stranger, haven't
you grown to be
like me
in your delight?

And all this
far too much
for any one of us. They
will go cold
and move on
the clustered figures
distilling the unknown
side of the park—

                        fecund, fortunate,
ravenous,
their production
dripping you spot by spot
towards a moment
identified perhaps
only afterwards.

And this sense of the shape
that comes to plug up
what you think of
yourself—
a performance—this
flexes through the
strained weight, momentarily
beaming, stretching
the chords and the walls
where air slips, as if
you were stung
by the anticipation
of it, built up out of
their desire to speak,
thirsting
for matter, for weeds
and recitations,
the representative form
hired to stand
before the class
every week, her
arching back,
how she would walk
between the easels.

For Paper Money

Isn't it odd isn't it
all odd

cold on my neck

here on the brink of clouds

would it be too far
to say I had earned
my space?

The full leaves
of my little tree
propped by the gray
window

Leaves on the tree
large like
features of a child

We are extravagant
ash,
hoarding forms

A landscape—is it
inexpensive?

architecture for

when are we less?
when are we more?

The Real and Unreal Mind

Nonspeech
is an action intricately
humming
So I waver

an unsubstantiated
avalanche of extras
to assuage

all split apart in this wind
still brisk enough to
separate from the skin

I scatter

and it moves
sharp, not biting
as in the pine needles

as in the engine
it makes
a different sound,

and also cloudy
like the shell of an ear
directing us inwards—I
scatter
as drips
reach near-constant
speed

the outer flowing
in a whine
of wires and all the wind chimes

interrupt

making this negative
space of tap
and slipping,

all this while
my hands hammering

the block of ice

There Is No Soul in the Subject Position

Your homeland struggles
to get away from you.

The curtain-folds
ripple, disclosing
in crescent marks
light of the afternoon.

I eat from the knife
asking, tell me
how you once were—

the windows won't say.
Now measures light on the blade.

Confucius Said "I Transmit, I Do Not Innovate"

They say he backed out
of the hall as if
contracting, withering
to use up less
air. He adjusted
a mat. Why why?
Articulation, he said,
is an outer form.
Meanness of motion
intercedes when we
walk into the warm spot
of an irony. Humor
cross cut with the passage
of time and the scribe's
error. The phrase, he said,
that you bring to bear
when this contraption
of words ensnares you
and some spring with glee
to be saved. But who
waits? The gentleman
swallows the tune
lest it be written down.
The notes fade
marvelously into the ashes—
the train
that circles momentarily
out of memory
then back into the room.

Love Song Variations

[AS SCHUMANN]

So twice the morning falls
into chinked key-spaces windows placid
gray of buildings opening New York
quiet and humble like the night was not before.

Here curtain-edges
palely dawning in swiveled motions
appeal to ambulatory innovation
laid out in fanned space—

the wild rumpled shirt of day
and its echoes: like two pianists echoing
and trilling one another, each at his own
well-tuned and black piano, that glares like a sleek

groomed buffalo, shaking off
crystal trinkets of water that a wooden concert hall
is made to thirst for and ponder dissolving.

[AS KURTÁG]

Brittle as the fool's gold
in your speed
faltering
                              the apartment, not invited

  drifts of paper bags
like ore.

Now to clang awake
                      with hotel bathroom glass
door, light

and London;

I won't go home to the ground floor
        so here

its all over listen no motives done
with my stupid optimism

in the dark
put on my glasses.

[AS DEBUSSY]

Like the camera lens there are no pictures just the flushing
water sound of the cool waiting and the wild optimistic plans.

4th of July where the restricted bay makes fireworks expand the sense
of place and small time well paid-for, and I left and sought you

stringing together haphazard idea after idea in the amphitheater
where we agreed on Brecht and walked in circles around

the rainy night to prove there could be no obstacle
and with weight of description approximated something sincere.

[AS BARTÓK]

On the grass experimenting

abstraction of the drummers' faces
wrongly switched

bodies arcing round the music
strongly taken, breaking in the

robes of black the war
of frame

in the grace of the measure
the march is

needling outward
nostalgia of the intrepid decades
chaos churning and fixing
the daft present of forms

and Conrad's double wakes next to him
in his bed and jumps back
into the sea

THE OIL RIG SESTINAS

Perdido Spar

It's out there, somewhere, staring from a horizon
200 miles offshore, in water too deep for conventional
tension legs. They call it *lost* as if from men,
from ourselves—from Dido? A gamble on breaking into currents
deeper below wet crusts of rock: this floating case of steel,
air, ballast, pressure, measured exactly—the welded chambers

channeling oil into the pipelines, pulling deep-chambered
algae and plankton from million-year mud: a time horizon
too far to follow but drilled open, cracked by steel
and by explosive charges. The method is unconventional—
imagined through three billion dollars in currents
of desperate technology that radiate agency out from men's

minds. Here master-slave arms uncouple from the men
who made them move uranium through glass chambers.
Now a sub-aqua rover glides, telemanipulated, between currents
as it tends to the wells: one video eye on the dark ultra-deep horizon
it returns lit images up to the platform where 150 conventional
bodies maintain a cramped equilibrium inside epoxy-painted steel,

held for two-week sessions within this coating ready to steal
heat from burning metal. The paint absorbs temperatures men
can't withstand—it bubbles and chars towards where conventional
bonds break and unstable electrons cut the layer cake chambers
down, melting. And whatever tropical disturbance covers the horizon
even then it is 2 hours flight 24 hours by boat through the currents

to any shore. How do I see this? Floating within the current
frame of cable-grids, invisible but embedded, I am made in habits of steel
I have never seen. I have sensed some tremor past the horizon
where flames follow the lines down—where creatures cluster like men
and drink chemosynthetically what wafts up from the oil chambers.

Fire follows, crossing into the sub-sea system, and conventional

sentiments are announced on the website, our conventions
of interests mount, their appetites pressing like the currents
that bring a shark far too deep—looking for food at our chamber's
very door—he rises inside the matrix of sub-aqua steel
installed over the submerged mountains: ranges that men
might never have seen, might have left dark, unbuilt upon, a horizon.

Disputed Site [Agbogbloshie E-Waste Center]

Listen. "It is the world's largest e-waste dump site."
Plastic encloses what men and kids patiently
dig for, scraping and burning what's brought
to this stretch in the center of Accra. Wiry
smoke rises from the mounds of the dump—
churns up and turns into soot clouds that pose

available for photographers to expose
this trash as our own. How best to see the sight
we're told is mostly our discarded monitors, the dump's
legal basis and central element, patented
cube seats and material drifting, inner wires
still unstripped. From containers brought

out of Europe, Australia, the US, often not *bought*
but *gifted*—"second-hand"—a practice now exposed
by journalists who tell us that our old wires
can be found here. But some say they're local. The site
shifts, sifts, while photos make their own patently
slanted stories. And the city's ordinary dumpsite

surrounds it all, showing us *the* wasteland dump-
scape we've imagined—as produce is brought
at dawn into the market next door. Where patient
sellers mind their stalls, abundance exposed
to air and ground and the long seep of this site
at the center of the city. As men gather wires

into bundles they guard all day then light into fires
that sear through the haze of the dump:
blossoms beckoning to those still rapt at the sight
of combustion and burn. Hydrogen chloride. Bought
for free like so much trash sorted and exposed

in this community improvising, at work, impatient—

attacked by some governments and important
media outlets—entities reaching out for the wires
in which user names are coiled sometimes exposed
then passed on to scammers who use what's dumped
in material no one thought to destroy. Stuff bought
and password-protected. Sent out of sight

from its source nation. Brought here now exposed
where the formerly unburdened consumer finds
his wires alive in a site of unmeasured impact.

Shipbreaking I: The Master Gas Cutter

You would not go there. Mountainous
ships gather in at the beach
of Alang. Each will feed 100 mouths
broken down into elements
by the young. Sent out between the places
we have scoured so now our harbors push it past

five countries, rusting, heaving a passage
along the sky—the man-made mountain
rubs against eternity. The hull displaces
water as the tanker rides in, beaches
at last in the shipyard: lot flooding when dark elemental
water runs over the workers' legs into the small mouths

of the mud and scattered metal, then flows out the mouth
of the harbor, settling. After its final passage
past the Cape this ship becomes scrap elements.
No more a merchant vessel. The captain
drops anchor, cuts power, steps down to the beach
and goes. The buyer's offshore money displaces

these now: multiple million dollars, a loan, and workers displaced
from poorer regions. Who cover their mouths
with cloth while one journalist climbs up from the beach
in blue body suit and full gas mask. He passes
into the bridge and points out the small mountains,
whitish piles of asbestos, each shred's harm an elemental

certainty. And iron. All around, the element's
ore mined from far grounds, forged into steel, displaced
in welded sheets and sent floating in the tumbling mountain
of tanker made steady with its great cavities of cargo. Tank mouths
sealed with ten miles of pipe and valves—the tons of oil that pass
sustaining nations, their corporate bodies held in the reach

of these cold quiet arms. But here where toxins leach
through oily mud workers run in this element
each day the tooled heat pours while summer passes
and hull sections crash—pulled apart in this place
where some still tower, announcing themselves like oaths
to bring distance up close, undissolved. Mountains

of want and labor. As the master gas cutter braces in this place
a country where the live gas line opens its small mouth
now his torch may cross igniting a mountain.

Border Station

The hat and the badge project a stable
selection of signs that overreach their functions.

The whites of eyes glisten off this excess
while elsewhere, out of range, destabilized data
withers into market ebullience—tunneling
attention through those accumulated icons

that have become the arena. Here all everyday iconic
interaction is insulated by this desert called stable

and free. Less and less resistant, the tunnels
carry more kinds of merchandise: a function
of retrenchment in the war against drugs and the data-
resistant attention applied, again, to the excess.

Still: the road is a place of transaction. Its excesses
are outlined, ready to make each conflict into an iconic

prize. Applicants on the other side arrange their data
aspirationally, drifting up on long, stable
lanes where everyone appears as a function
of insufficiency. They move towards an image, a tunnel

to somewhere—while the sight of this barrier tunnels
into their minds, expressing the wait for access

that claims all the days. This overseen by the function
of simulators: gripping equipment that unifies its icons
of obstruction, consolidates surroundings with stable
lapel cameras, tracking coordinators, conflict data

implemented for full-force situations. The data-
collecting system that maps private spaces which tunnel

away from the borders: as in, one school photo, stabilized
by tape in a split-level beside which a permanent excess
of cars extends sonorous—even now they are still icons
of something with their drip-drip gait, their functioning

less and less ideal. Here where listening bodies function
as solid spaces, grooving the wide land, *their* data

hovers in erasures they weave through an icon—
a country they cannot enter where everyday tunnels
shift now, no place but still a tactile region of weaponized excess,
a bleached blossom, an atomized laugh that cannot stabilize

or be absorbed, its functions synthesized out of red games
distorting all data, the excess of icons unstable,
spurious in ongoing dispute, a raging tunnel to nowhere.

Foreign Wars

A house within the water: within
it a house. Our compressed bulwark. Tidal
raiment of many bodies, hemmed with proof,
like a railing. One line of defenses
plumbs no depths but presses
outward, a sun-stretched film, a fin.

This is the set—the stage to make tides fully fin
-like, arousing the currents within
imagination—currents that turn upon pressed
lips, dredging the somnolent tides
of heavy, balletic defenses
away from their flaxen notions of proof—

like cloud-cover, these draw over the roofs
unleashing opalescent fins
across the district which is almost defenseless
as it watches the sea without preparing in
even its own small way for the tides
that shift and shiver but still press

on like a news channel, a glib presenter
catching the common tone: the proofs
that these are not just one-time tides
that pour seductively, stroking their thick fins
along this coast with their incredible
weight, but the metallic gleam of defense

mechanisms—oiled machine-defenses
that raise amphibious limbs to press
on past the beach, towards a pin
deep in the heat-map, a central proof
of this action. Our fingers
leap up out of the tides:

an army that masses, its training a tidal
repertoire of muscular scales, defenses
harbored and harboring motion, the fins
of muscle hold and release and press
patterns of code: a woven structure in
which human weight is a wasted proof.

I Got This: At the LinkNYC Wi-Fi Kiosk

1/
To capture the tipping action
I try holding my tension tighter.
Hurry with yearning up to the kiosk
I get stuck pressing into the keys
with my [look] but all interests
seem to fall [out] spread pinging and feigned.

2/
This rummaging surplus of feigned
minutes tries itself silly sweeping action
over the fences of sly interest
[while] who's [weeping] inside the scrimmage tighter
than ever, its angel holds out key
options and proffers them at the kiosk.

3/
I'm still trying to catch [up to] that kiosk
how I approached it on the avenue feigning
grace. Under my skin the square keys
impress one calculated transaction
involved with moving farther. Tighter
steps that cut and bounce the [feeling of] interest

4/
accumulating. Lobbyist interests
strain at my command of the kiosk
its knowledge of what I want tightening
around the scale the walls the dog feigning
happiness on our walk, a [possible] reaction
to the coded presence of keys.

5/

Recently computing the same key
[structures] their limelight set of interested
investors and problematic actions
indefinite, set in motion when the kiosk
pounds out a halting problem, feigned
for the purpose of preparations, all this tightening

6/

at the entry [point.] Path-dependent tightening
fixes the 0-computable key
more worst-case execution time feigned
than swallowed: all parties with interest
but no transformation: their kiosk's
range still stagnant: programmed set of actions

7/

all inputs act on termination, tighter
than the kiosk's plan, its trigger keys
laid open for your feigned interest.

Stoma

Spring changes what it's made of, the air
loosening, tree fibers warming while new
light-frequencies press brimming over the root zones
damaged in winter. The trunk holds but its axis
tilts tipping a canopy that dandles leaves
to inhale over troughs of rich chemical

air. Inside each leaf, flights of swirling-in chemical
carbon dioxide—fast and thin. Wisping into the airy
underside stomata cells of these leaves
that entertain, allow access to interiors newly
awakened when earth tilted its old axis
curtailing the night. Then within this temperate zone

the phytochrome—sensitive to far-red zones
of the visual spectrum—presses chemical
fingers into the small branches, triggers a praxis
of bud-building that spins sugars shaken out of the air
and folds them into tiny bud-newspapers
wound up, bound, bundled, soon to become leaves.

Flooded with blossoms—is this how nature leaves
us? The tree all in heat, blustering into the warm zones
of the airspace, demonstrating a readiness in its sinews
for reproduction it fizzes up pink like some chemical
toxin. These limbs are as delicate as ever, debonair
though laden, arraying their plunder out from that axis

the trunk whose seed fell down here like a taxi
passenger deposited by accident. The leaves
regrow. They don't know how to despair
as now the branches with their flailing arms emblazon
the sky, claiming the air where new chemical
compounds waft over a property whose contract renews

while its prospects decay. I am newly
infused with boundaries this spring, watching the tree's axis
slant, crossing the land, spreading its earthy alchemical
vision. A villain says, nobody leaves
until I say so, but this time his interzone
of ownership extends into but one cross-section of airspace.

The tree is dying. I know. Still pressing new buds up
from its axis, its leaves catch at vitreous air.
The stoma tugs at clear space. The chemical sky divides.

Shipbreaking II: They Sell the Steel

Who stays on the ships so long?
Up in chambers gripped
by cables men haul
out on human lines. The snaked steel weight
drags over the beach—out from winch
that hooks these tons of nature

and pulls them back, broken. To the creature-
like curves of this hull the gas cutter brings his long
study of metal structures. He guides the winch's
work—acetylene torch in his grip
he cuts a small door and enters where fire weighs
so little held in his hands all day as he hauls

attention through his mind now all
danger glares there ready to burst while nature
spreads chance unsteady through weight
of hurry exhaustion and darkness of long
overtime—he can't see what steel shadows grip
space through the smoke and the winch

continuously tugging as each inch
of cable must pass cleanly, the operators all
observing the machine how its inhuman grip
startles metal mountains out of their natural
tensions which tremble now straining the long
heavy lines that buckle when weight

twists unpredictably into new cuts not waiting
to fall in orderly fashion here away from the winch
which only loves what is ferrous—the long
joints weak all at once now all
in motion the walls collapse into or out of nature
these sheets and pinions that may grip

men out of their lives—the gas cutters still gripping
their torches leap sometimes too late away from weight
they must calculate with no diagram as teacher
of what they break: grand blocks each inch
drawn decades ago made in a drydock where all
their architecture hung suspended between long

cables, the load susceptible to wind for long
seconds when the shipyard fell silent in the grip
of thousands of tons drifting over it all.
Time schedules trade value contracts contract into weight
the fact each human feels guiding the block to one inch
of ground where it must land, gaining new stature

as ship that knows nothing of chance or creatures
who may consider the near-infinite reactions of long
days months years of exposure to stench
toxins fire eyes dimming while others may grip
onto their lives pull back into the steadier weight
of the yard, a beach where large pieces hauled

in are separated and cut down called
finally out from their ships these battered features
diminish sorted by thickness quality and weight
old scarred shapes that vanish along
the yard where the large pieces flatten gripped
by workers who cut out sheets the winch

will move again, now into piles the winch
supervisor organizes for loaders to haul
onto trucks to sell downstream to industries gripped
by the hunger to build with what nature
can't provide here where mills reroll long
molten rods of metal spit out each in weight

length size perfect glowing orange straight
collecting and cooling their standard inches

that go contracted into the city's long
avenues and within each apartment hauled
up, lords and ladies, steel brought out of nature
into the air, these skeletal frames into whose grip

the gas cutters do not come, but others hauled to this high bough
gripped by the weight of the body, that steady winch
in which they have grown tired for so long.

AFTER THE SUBLIME OBJECT

America

1
When you get an idea here
it's like keeping a memory.
The scene completed before
you pierce the stickered tissue
stark and full of clearness.

2
To capture the tipping point
there is a backdrop of dark
city—bridges, the high
buildings that warp in the labyrinth.

Like a comic book's veiled romance
blindness contrasts the visible gray.

3
What happens is always
after and exhausted. Limelight
appearing
to appear behind the lifestyle scene.

4
So many bright organisms complicate
the shadows.

5
My citizenship a possible
speech bubble around here
somewhere broad enough so
you wonder what place
could you could pin it on

maybe even a totem of
this scepter still falling
still this thing.

Borderlands

1:

Is it this country
where we will share the land?

The days are always like yesterday
the sun too mild

and withheld, though we divert it
through our yards, speeding

tubes into our chambers.
We will divide the desert cleanly

and visit sometimes. Like
a lesser friend, and remember

it in ourselves—our veins
of gold, and happy

that midday impresses these
again into the camera.

Yes, I will look out
and see what I meant to see.

Three tributaries, one
must flood, and we'll find it

rushing: its desert
dark mud-wash lapping blanket over—

2:

the infinite color
in some sort of danger.

Is this an image?
From the light sprays in the dry
surface prepared for movement—

Is this an image
of the indented desert?

The light sprays in the dry dirt, the wisps
of stray grasses carried tumbling
on the top of water,
a froth on the waters

dark mud lapping its blanket over—
its cables of soft perforated grit

molding the levels, scores in the basin—

grit collecting where some seeds must tumble,
abraded, in order to sprout

when the waters fold
where the dry topsoil crumbles and folds

and the tributary and its seed
into and under the gray-red water

come, imagine
now I am gone

dark mud lapping its blanket over—

How I Loved the 20th Century

I enter this scene
sweeping, with a little
hat on.
Three strokes
to the left, three
to the right, I mimic
your innuendo your
conversation
the swarm
of your small grace
played out
in the syntax
packed, unwinding
its inevitable rhythm.

I polish the lens of this overture,
I polish the floor of this defiance.

This is the final intuition.

This form of the mountain—
the form of its mountainous
logic

that must suckle, scour,
be scoured—

the floor of this plate
clean, untouched,
ready for greed.

I enter, I can enter.

Watch me.

I bow at the door.

Form Eroding on the Nogales to Phoenix Route

An animal senses a
darker-than-shadow
distortion within the
wide mesmerizing sand.

Where gravel tumbles
and dry water
drowns green in ochre,
the dry water left to stand.

Smudging the sand with their soft-
covered shoes
the carriers nimble
over gravel.

The pure product bundled,
then gallons
painted darker than shadows
that pass over quick, invisible roots.

Painted darker than shadows
the gallons, somewhere
where runners leave them
between the coarse open bands

of the earth—that product
tumbles in low, collecting
somewhere where runners leave
green drowned in ochre,

smudging the sand.

The Subject Vanishes

i
Where we live
in the bomb

the sprout of the bomb
is with us

ii
the sprout of our received
believing—ourselves

built in a seed
from loose ground.

iii
At its edges, elements
corrode our structure's

semi-porous
walls. Fingers dig

in the grime
and the grime becomes

ridges of our skins. So

be it. Of the fruit
we know only what

we are told

by those who see
our faces

iv
Desire
will cut you off—

what you describe
compacted

longing to grip
trash you cannot take

in and where
desire holds, it cuts:

it holds and it cuts

v
remember how

change, this scabbard
was meant to move
slowly

yet nails fly
from the imagination

vi
what moves (from the dark, in the chaos
first) as the crowd flushes

the flesh in its soft rain

vii
it severs
and on this stem

harm
glitters anew

FROM GARBAGE

The Great Pacific Garbage Patch Speaks

i.

I have seen myself.
My limbs my specks my dots of organs
afloat. Sometimes a planet rumbles
overhead and its weight like a road
touches me. I remember the land.
I remember those shores
where my items formed
so light as to be almost lifeless.

The ocean sings also.
I drift coordinated
in currents that spin slowly—
my vortex—a million
humming items that travel
under the surface
as gyre and subgyre pull
what into their loop—what size—
what surviving subset of particles
together churning—

ii.

I know nothing
about my little fears. Single use
items fragile when the body
wakes to wind
through all my cavities.

My riches shift and I know
I am not an island
but eddies—what is flushed

out from rivers—

out of the Yangtze,
Indus, Amur, Mekong—
out of the Nile—

iii.

This refuse
of the land's great need.
Its plastics, bellows,
bleached nets.

There were fingers
once on the ribs of this bottle—
this twangling organ—what

on land was a container,
a containing.

There form
is a monster of indecision.
And these are the remnants—tooled marks
from the factory—threads
on the neck—and I flee

out into the open: I skim,
spreading where light shines
& salt feasts & I burn
& parch & time
takes over my bodies. I sag

and gravity pulls
the mouth up, holds
these great plastic opportunities—

what is concave
what is convex

what floats
what is sumptuous
what is frayed
what is gone
what pecks you and tugs—

then tunnels take you
the water turns
and your blood is just a small drop
of iron, it will dry
even in the ocean—

iv.

When containers break open—

fear this—there is no
island—then there is
an island—delight
you will never have—sometimes

voices call, holding
riches up

this veneer of plastic—

flesh of confetti—

there is no pain but
sometimes a thousand sounds

will show what I can't imagine

how I touch

toxic excitement

partially crystalline

never becoming
something you know

I rotate
over my bodies
seeking dispersal

I peel myself—

help me
is not a thought
let it fail
melting through the skin
of each container
this is not an island
spreading in the water

Notes from the Northwest Incinerator
(Concerning the Progress of the Ship KHIAN SEA)

i.

What was the Northwest Incinerator,

    I am. Ash-only piles:

    heavy metals mobilized—

    dropped as turbidity into waters

    and easily brought airborne—

ii.

I know that ashes
are unwanted
but I want them—I feel

men cleaning me,
taking up more
to make into value

but Wayne, why
are they driving
away evidence, soft

sponging memory
pulled out, burned off
the grid—I need

to keep what we
recovered, emitted,
expelled—hold it on site

in words that name

my 14,000 tons

of weight—their taking it

elsewhere

    iii.

My ash sailed out
on a contract—

they changed the boat's
name, rechristened
its cargo—

for two years
they've carried the ash—
they tip

      4,000 tons

      onto the beach
      near Gonaïves—

      wind-blown

      refuse

catches the air—

the locals say it's killing

their goats—

iv.

So I linger, I pass

no longer
large or odiferous—

sent on over the ocean—

It has to do with
compliance: ash

stretching out
of perjury
and down under water

>> where what's burned
>> spreads in materials
>> not yet inert

and the words

blunder—then

>> one crewmember
>> begs on the beach:

>> he says "no danger"

>> to a camera

>> he begs
>> by eating ash—

v.

Night advanced—

no one sees

where I spread—

men move

with my corpse, unhoused

and this extends up
out of it—what emerges

in wild flowers, in small
pine trees—

this is where I stoop

this is where I stoop

before or after
expectation

when ash drops down—opens

under the foil

of the ocean

Injection Molding // Whale Fall

*In Shenzhen. The plastic injection molding machine considers itself, with
reference to the way whales sink when they die in the ocean.*

No tool to tell you

how the whale sinks down.

I become renewable,

without loss,

hoping to stop in time.

      *

Each day the new
protagonist is here

in the factory. Billiard balls
in hot plastic. Molded parts asking

how do I sink in the sea?
can you show me?

      *

I ignore this. Still wondering

      how does the whale fall—

      the original whale—

      his great bones crushing down...

*

One whale body
will equal 2,000 springtimes

arriving

through more than an instant.

Muscles tip out
from spine—parachute

to the deep sea floor—

*

where no tool

may register how his death
spread in the dark.

How it multiplied
where fathoms loosen,

joints unfolding.

*

I stretch into
a shape. Do as I'm told

in plastics. Each mold

is a house
is an ocean but

only now do I know
his death was never some renewable

substance. The whale sank away—

out of contact,

and what they wanted me for

was to make more stuffs,
billiard balls,

toys

that would bounce
properly.

*

People invented
the paper bag. Invented
glass bottle factories. I tried

to measure my senses.

But there was only the sea
of my sinking: flushed

outflow. Products
marked by ejector pins—

stamps remembering the mold

pressed off after plastic pellets

melted in heat,

reformed.

*

Am still restricted. Smell

traducing these stairs, hot

force in the vents. I house

and unhouse—not knowing

what they send down

and out through me.

      *

I am especially spread out

among 600,000 whales sinking now

across the ocean. They wanted

some renewable substance.

And no tool ready

to make more remembering.

      *

Am alive

in great boxes that crush

down through the mammal.

Stuck inside

      as an anecdote

the bells and whistles
whole greenhouses
with watering can, plastic plates and cups—
all of it falling, all of it the dead
protagonist

who enters the ocean

unprepared.

*

Still sketch a shape

sometimes. Become that shape, repeating.

What they began to invent

with ivory imaginations. Colonial characters

bound up on small

pages. Production which

is not just some marine snow

releasing its shadow.

*

Take perspective
and turn it.

The thinking body is

materials. Potential energy.

To have an emotion.

And wasn't I the whale

sometimes?

                    *

If springtime

is a disgrace, I am still

here

through all the senses—how

the parachute escapes

off the whale—its muscle—and I

am angry, turbulent

crossing unusual smells

after ejector pins rock me

from the surface—I

detach

from the mold—an anecdote

is forming around

myself. a house. the gate

built without any true

sense of the mammal or

smell of sea—when after all

what people wanted was

the game to go on

forever, the billiard balls

to bounce into pockets—this

is not an essay it is not

efficient, sinking

like a gift—then what

can come up to me, to my side

down here, in little clicks

and vibrations—lacerations, potential

of hope—when smells move outward

creatures sense this

springtime arriving

where I stretch

into the story

of seen things. a staircase

still passing downwards—

these marks my measure,

gate of ejector pins,

a witness—here

where the ocean holds

this bland mark

The Kola Superdeep Borehole Waits

i.

Lodged down
        in earth's crust, I wonder

what is air? A breath
        beneath my plate bolted down.
The air, bolted down.
        If I lift through it
I might become
        a thousand other organisms—
might diffuse into
        an interplanetary zone
of open wind.

ii.

And the air up there
        could be gathered like a child.
Density alive like I was
        when drills pressed
through arctic crust,
        burrowed burning
into my area
        that swells, whole, frozen
above earth's mantle.

iii.

Now what's left is some shadow,
        cooling. Semblance of a question
about resources
        within the slow expansive waves
of the planet—

an impression.
        Tethered to it, I
        can't see into the open,
        what the open becomes.

When here is just a breath
bolted down:

        if I lift through it
what I enter is only
        a container made
        in thought
        by separation.

        iv.

What speaks is a created nothing.
Path in minerals.
A hard memory.

It was 1970.

In the Arctic USSR
under a sky filled with random hum
they began drilling.

My behavior is only an echo

of their equipment

which behaved properly

on most days.

v.

They found water
and they were glad.

They found
single-celled organisms.

They took the fossils out
in cores—

vi.

And still I seek myself out, a place
within history.

It is an action of familiarity,
how I extend
towards an aerial world.

I study the evidence
from insects. The way air fluctuates
in viruses, fungus and spores
a thousand meters above the surface—

and if I wait I must be like
snowfields stained yellow, red, or green
with the action of bacteria.

vii.

I am only a hum that is moving.

viii.

A rain.

Seismic waves.

Turbulent imagining

of all the summers of history.

What spreads in flowing rock
that melts the drill lines.

When up there are the snowfields.

And what have I made.

Miles of earth.

Ice rings broken by wind.

A thousand miles.

An hour.

The living rain.

When restless motion writes me

above the land's surface. Where I

examine the habitat that I am. I break

from the heat that is lifting.

What is alive.

NOTES

"Notes from the Northwest Incinerator" makes reference to the ship *Khian Sea*, which departed from the port of Philadelphia in 1986. The *Khian Sea* carried over 14,000 tons of solid ash waste— the product of a local facility called the Northwest Incinerator. When rumors of the ash's toxicity spread, the ship was turned away from the Bahamas and from the ports of eleven other countries. The crew dumped most of the ash along the ship's route through the ocean.

"The Kola Superdeep Borehole Waits" makes reference to a scientific drilling project conducted in the Soviet Union between 1970 and 1995. In 1979 the Kola Superdeep Borehole became the deepest man-made hole on earth.

ACKNOWLEDGEMENTS

My gratitude goes to the editors of the following journals, in which the poems in this book first appeared:

American Poetry Review: "America," "At the Hotel," "Desire," "Borderland" and "The Subject Vanishes"

Colorado Review: "Chassis Excavation," "Concave/Convex," and "Touch Screen"

Conjunctions: "Shipbreaking," "Stoma," "Disputed Site [Agbogbloshie E-Waste Center]," and "Perdido Spar"

Denver Quarterly: "Room" and "Sustain"

Peripheries: "The Great Pacific Garbage Patch Speaks"

Poetry Daily: "America"

Web Conjunctions: "Ceremonial Dialogue With the Feng Tripod," "Collage," "Love Song Variations," "The Notion of Originality," "The Real and Unreal Mind," "Injection Molding // Whale Fall," and "Notes from the Northwest Incinerator"

The Yale Review: "For Paper Money"

I am deeply grateful to my teachers, especially Jorie Graham, Xiaofei Tian, Stephen Owen, Leslie Brisman, Robert Reed, Louise Glück, and Lyn Vlaskamp. I would also like to thank Bradford Morrow, Donald Revell, John T. Hamilton, David Der-wei Wang, Christopher Johnson, and Teju Cole for their generosity and mentorship.

I am grateful to the Harvard Creative Writing Program and to my extraordinary workshop colleagues, especially Tim McGinnis, Sherah Bloor, Aditya Menon, Zoë Hitzig, Adrienne Raphel, Angelo Mao, Amanda Gunn, Isabel Duarte-Gray, Christopher Spaide, and Julian Gewirtz.

Thank you to Martin Quinn for his brilliance, insight, and support during the years when these poems were written.

Thank you to my family and to Laura Adler, Rachel Rose, Michael Pinkham, Ben Harwood, Jesús Castillo, and Parker Phillips.

Finally, thank you to Matthew Pennock and to Robert L. Giron and Ken Schellenberg at Gival Press.

ABOUT THE AUTHOR

Kate Monaghan lives in New York City. Her poems have appeared in the *American Poetry Review*, *Conjunctions*, the *Yale Review*, and elsewhere. She holds a BA in Studio Art and English from Yale and a PhD in classical Chinese poetry from Harvard.

Photo by Jesús I. Castillo.

POETRY FROM GIVAL PRESS

Abandoned Earth by Linwood D. Rumney

Adama: Poème / Adama: Poem by Céline Zins with English translation by Peter Schulman

Architects of the Imaginary / Los arquitectos de lo imaginario by Marta López-Luaces with translation by G. J. Racz

Bones Washed in Wine: Flint Shards from Sussex and Bliss by Jeff Mann

Box of Blue Horses by Lisa Graley

Camciones para una sola cuerda / Songs for a Single String by Jesús Gardea with English translation by Robert L. Giron

Dervish by Gerard Wozek

Disputed Site by Kate Monaghan

The Great Canopy by Paula Goldman

Grip by Yvette Neisser Moreno

Haint by Teri Ellen Cross Davis

Honey by Richard Carr

Let Orpheus Take Your Hand by George Klawitter

Leave Smoke by Jeff Walt

Metamorphosis of the Serpent God by Robert L. Giron

Meteor by C. M. Mayo

Museum of False Starts by Chip Livingston

On the Altar of Greece by Donna J. Gelagotis Lee

On the Tongue by Jeff Mann

Poetic Voices Without Borders edited by Robert L. Giron

Poetic Voices Without Borders 2 edited by Robert L. Giron

Prosody in England and Elsewhere: A Comparative Approach by Leonardo Malcovati

Protection by Gregg Shapiro

Psaltery and Serpentines by Cecilia Martínez-Gil

Refugee by Vladimir Levchev

The Miracle Machine by Matthew Pennock

The Nature Sonnets by Jill Williams

The Origin of the Milky Way by Barbara Louise Ungar

The Silent Art by Clifford Bernier

Some Wonder by Eric Nelson

Songs for the Spirit by Robert L. Giron

Sweet to Burn by Beverly Burch

Tickets for a Closing Play by Janet I. Buck

Twelve: Sonnets for the Zodiac by John Gosslee

Voyeur by Rich Murphy

We Deserve the Gods We Ask For by Seth Brady Tucker

Where a Poet Ought Not / Où c'qui faut pas by G. Tod Slone

For a complete list of Gival Press titles, visit: www.givalpress.com.
Books available from Ingram, Brodart, Follett, your favorite
bookstore, on-line booksellers, or directly from Gival Press.

Gival Press, LLC
PO Box 3812
Arlington, VA 22203
givalpress@yahoo.com
703.351.007

CPSIA information can be obtained
at www.ICGtesting.com
Printed in the USA
JSHW020800121122
33003JS00003B/159